I0207978

The Simple Secret
Study Guide

The Simple Secret
Study Guide

Choosing Love in a Culture of Hostility

KIM SHAFFER KIRKMAN

CASCADE *Books* • Eugene, Oregon

THE SIMPLE SECRET STUDY GUIDE
Choosing Love in a Culture of Hostility

Copyright © 2025 Kim Shaffer Kirkman. All rights reserved. Except for brief quotations in critical publications or reviews, no part of this book may be reproduced in any manner without prior written permission from the publisher. Write: Permissions, Wipf and Stock Publishers, 199 W. 8th Ave., Suite 3, Eugene, OR 97401.

Cascade Books
An Imprint of Wipf and Stock Publishers
199 W. 8th Ave., Suite 3
Eugene, OR 97401

www.wipfandstock.com

PAPERBACK ISBN: 979-8-3852-0673-5
HARDCOVER ISBN: 979-8-3852-0674-2
EBOOK ISBN: 979-8-3852-0675-9

Cataloguing-in-Publication data:

Names: Kirkman, Kim Shaffer, author.

Title: The simple secret study guide : choosing love in a culture of hostility / Kim Shaffer Kirkman.

Description: Eugene, OR: Cascade Books, 2025 | Includes bibliographical references.

Identifiers: ISBN 979-8-3852-0673-5 (paperback) | ISBN 979-8-3852-0674-2 (hardcover) | ISBN 979-8-3852-0675-9 (ebook)

Subjects: LCSH: Love—Religious aspects—Christianity. | Study guide.

Classification: BV4639 K57 2025 (paperback) |BV4639 (ebook)

07/28/25

This study guide is dedicated to my husband, Brett,
for loving me so well.

"Love is our true destiny. We do not find the meaning of life by ourselves alone—we find it with another."

—THOMAS MERTON

"Love the Lord your God with all your heart, all your soul, and all your mind. This is the first and most important command. And the second command is like the first: 'Love your neighbor as yourself.'"

—MATTHEW 22:37–39 NCV

Contents

Acknowledgments		ix
Dear Reader		1
1	Love Is the Meaning of Life	3
2	Loving God	6
3	Loving Humans	9
4	Loving Myself	13
5	Loving Partners	15
6	Loving Children	18
7	Loving Friends	21
8	Loving the Vulnerable	23
9	Loving the Poor	26
10	Loving Strangers	29
11	Loving Enemies	32
12	Only Love Can Set You Free	34
Bonus Chapter: Loving Parents		37
Bibliography		41

Acknowledgments

In the spring of 2023, *The Simple Secret*, by Joshua Graves, was published.

I texted him. "Are you planning to have a study guide? I plan to use this book with my college group in the fall and would love to have it for my preparation."

Josh answered, "That is incredibly kind, and I really appreciate it . . . A few people have asked about a study guide. Here's a crazy idea . . . What if you wrote it? I'm being serious."

I got his reply while leading my weekly team meeting. I saw the message but could not respond immediately.

A few minutes later, Josh replied: "Bad idea?"

When I could respond I wrote: "Good idea!"

Over the next few days, we had a couple of conversations about what this could look like, and then I got to work.

On one of those calls, I asked Josh, "Why did you ask *me* to write the study guide?"

Josh said, "I felt the Spirit nudging."

This was a challenging project and deeply encouraging for me. Thank you, Josh, for listening to the Spirit and asking me to collaborate with your work.

In the spring of 2024, I led a community group in Searcy, Arkansas, through the book using this study guide. Many people shared with me their personal growth during this study.

I pray that you will be challenged and moved to growth during this study and that your group will have the experience to build a deeper community.

Dear Reader,
This study will transform your life (if you let it) and how you think about *every* person in your world.

"For God so loved the world that he gave his only begotten son that whosoever believes in him will have eternal life."[1]

A familiar verse—that is heard and seen on billboards worldwide. Love. The topic of popular songs and poetry has been around for centuries. So much has been written about it. We long to find love, to be in it, to feel it, and to give it. We are wonderfully created to search for it from birth.

"They [newborns] are searching with an instinct far deeper than intention. They are looking for a face, and when they find one—especially a face that gazes back at them, they fix their eyes on it, having found what they were most urgently looking for."[2]

Introduction

As you prepare to use this guide and book to lead a group, several things are worth your consideration.

- First, you may have read *The Simple Secret* and now are preparing to lead a group, or you may be starting this book based on recommendations to use it and are reading/preparing one chapter at a time.

- The second consideration is whether you will be the only one reading *The Simple Secret* or may be leading a guided discussion in a book club-type group.

1. John 3:16.
2. Crouch, "Life We're Looking For," 72–73.

The Simple Secret Study Guide

Although it can be profitably used by an individual, solo reader, this study guide has been prepared especially with groups in mind. However your group is organized, this guide is designed to provide the best opportunity for thoughtful discussion of the content. Your preparation time is valuable; the goal is to give you the tools for the best outcomes.

As you begin, consider your goals for this study. Reflecting and planning the goals will prime your study for growth.

- What do you hope to develop through *The Simple Secret* in your group?
- How will you measure if you have achieved this with your group?

Pray for the gift of teaching through this study, and be open to the Holy Spirit's nudging.

The first four foundational chapters deal with the love of life, God, humanity, and ourselves. These pillar chapters are best used in that order. Based on your group demographics, the other chapters' order may be rearranged as you see fit. I added a bonus chapter. I am a season ahead of Josh in life and shared a little about my personal experiences of loving our aging parents. It is too raw for me to include siblings, as I am navigating some challenging times in dealing with my mother's journey.

Additional readings are recommended with each chapter, and a complete resource listing is included at the end. There is a link to a presentation of this study guide to see if that format is helpful to your study.

I am confident that this study will bless you, and I pray that all who prepare to teach and lead a group will be blessed exponentially.

Kim Shaffer Kirkman, EdD

PS Keep a journal of this journey. Encourage your group to keep a journal, too.

1

Love Is the Meaning of Life

Who are *your* people when you think about life, and who are you walking beside now?

How does Jesus fit into your thinking?

In the busyness of living, we often start at chapter 1 when reading a new book or preparing for study.

Read Josh's acknowledgments and Introduction. He sets the stage for the entire book and gives insight into his inspiration for this book. I often read aloud to my students. There are sometimes ways to share things in your own words, and at other times, the author's words are best. Josh writes:

> Jesus taught me how to love every kind of person I've ever encountered. It's really extraordinary when you slow down to consider. I learned the most important lessons about life from a Jewish itinerant preacher who lived two thousand years ago halfway around the world. He didn't speak English. He never heard of America, the Dallas Cowboys, English Premier League soccer, or Michael Jackson. Yet, Jesus was, without question, the best and most important thing that has happened to me.[1]

1. Graves, *Simple Secret*, 3.

THE SIMPLE SECRET STUDY GUIDE

Have the group take note of Scot McKnight's surgical definition of love, which is precisely on point. "Love is a rugged commitment to be with someone, to be for someone unto Christ's likeness for as long as it takes."[2]

Share Oliver's wet kiss story.[3] It's endearing and what we all yearn to hear. You may have a personal experience to share. Your group may be already connected and free to share personal experiences. If your group is new, give them time. Later in the study, you can return to this story and have a chance to share in more depth.

What does love require of me?

Share your thoughts.

Over the next few weeks, we will explore "loving" in all the relational facets life presents.[4]

Think about a time in your life when you felt most loved. It is hard to pick and narrow it down to one, if you are like me. It might be after a long illness, your wedding, or time with a grandparent. It may have been after a long separation from a dear friend.

I can recall times I felt loved. A few weeks after my daddy passed away from an illness, my brother discovered a file of Daddy's filled with letters for each of his six living children and my mother. I waited until I was alone to read my letter. I always felt unconditional love from my daddy and felt a little nervous about reading his last written words to me. We did not know he had written these love letters. It turns out he had written each one a few days before he had bladder cancer surgery, and we would find the notes eighteen months after that surgery. He did not know if he would survive the surgery and have a chance to say he loved us. This letter today sits in the top drawer of my bedside table. It was an unexpected gift and now a treasured gift. I know it's there and feel his love when I read his words. He passed away in 2014. I reread his letter regularly and feel deeply loved. It is also why I periodically write love letters to my people. With each letter I write, I realize that it may be my last letter to them.

2. McKnight, "Four Elements of Love."
3. Graves, *Simple Secret*, 6–7.
4. Graves, *Simple Secret*, 10.

LOVE IS THE MEANING OF LIFE

"Love is a daily decision to be tenaciously aware and attentive to the needs of others around you."[5]

Read: 1 Corinthians 13:1–13.

A few months ago, my husband Brett and I attended a small conference for writers in San Diego. Going to San Diego in February was a gift to our souls. I had surprised Brett with the conference and decided to go along to see what it was all about. I expected Brett to kick-start his writing and saw my role as an encourager. I was surprised by the experience that I had. And we both returned to our winter weather in Arkansas feeling refreshed and motivated.

One unexpected blessing was meeting Sweet Maria (IYKYK: Bob Goff's endearing name for his wife). I purchased Maria's book and later looked at her inscription, "Kim, Love lives in you!" Her work is a beautiful collection of love stories: "The same power that dug Jesus out of a cave can unearth beautiful things in our lives, too."[6]

Journal:

- Remember feeling completely loved: Everything. Write how it felt, sounded, and smelled. Don't judge or scrutinize yourself.
- Who's there?
- What do you see?
- What's happening?
- What is spoken?
- How do you feel?
- What is unspoken but felt?

5. Graves, *Simple Secret,* 14.
6. Goff, *Love Lives Here,* 79.

2

Loving God

Take a moment to think about the important people in your life. Write their names here.

Family	Friends
Romance	All-in-love (Agape)

LOVING GOD

Slowing down to name important loved ones is one way that we maintain a grateful disposition for these gifts from God.

There is a member of your family who matters a great deal to you. You have a friend who's likely closer than family. You are either in or coming out of a romantic-connection relationship. You probably have someone you sacrifice for on a daily basis.[1]

Our language does not have adequate words for love. We have to borrow from the Greeks, which is hard to understand. We have heard stories, lessons, and perhaps sermons all trying to give us meaning for the Greek words in English.

Family love: *Storge*

Friend love: *Phileo*

Romantic love: *Eros*

All-in-love: *Agape*

We are familiar with English words that have been created from these Greek meanings:

Philadelphia: the city of brotherly love

Erotic: tending to arouse sexual love (which makes us a little nervous reading this here)

Agape: the name of churches, adoption agencies, etc.

Familial love, *storge*, has yet to enter our language as the other three have.

Jesus was asked, tested really, by the teachers of the law[2] as to what was the most important of all the commandments. Remember, the Torah is full of laws for everything—eating, drinking, doing, not doing—more than I can wrap my mind around. No wonder there was a sacrifice for unintentional sins if you violated one of these hundreds of laws.[3]

Jesus answered, "The most important one is the Shema: 'Hear O Israel; The Lord our God, the Lord is one. Love the Lord, your God, with all your heart, and with all your soul, and with all your

---

1. Graves, *Simple Secret*, 22.

2. Mark 12:28–34.

3. Lev 4.

THE SIMPLE SECRET STUDY GUIDE

mind, and all your strength. The second is this: 'Love your neighbor as yourself.' There is no commandment greater than these."[4]

So, what does Jesus do here? He gives us what is most important. Love God and love people. "It's how we change the world."[5]

The story Josh shares on page 23 about Richard and Andy is beautiful. Read it aloud to share love in action.

Journal:

- Look at the list of the people you love. A quote in Josh's book hits us right between the eyes. "Who do you love the least on that list?"[6]

- Is that how much you love God?

- Reflect on this: In *Love Does,* Bob Goff clearly states, "We'd know the extent of our love for God by how well we loved people."[7]

---

4. Mark 12:29.

5 Gokey, "Love God and Love People."

6. Graves, *Simple Secret,* 35.

7. Goff, *Love Does,* 15.

3

Loving Humans

Jesus saw humans. He saw people hurting, lonely, hungry—for food and love. How do you see humans?

I regularly see a man standing on the corner with a sign, "Anything will help."

What do I do with that? Anything? Maybe I offer five dollars from my wallet, or a package of peanut butter crackers.

I want to help. I want to see people like Jesus did. The traffic is heavy. The light is changing.

I look away with an ache of missing the opportunity.

I was hungry, and you gave me food. I was thirsty, and you gave me something to drink. I was alone and away from home, and you invited me into your house. I was without clothes, and you gave me something to wear. I was sick, and you cared for me. I was in prison, and you visited me. "Then the good people will answer, 'Lord, when did we see you hungry and give you food, or thirsty and give you something to drink? When did we see you alone and away from home and invite you into our house? When did we see you without clothes and give you something to wear? When did we see you sick or in prison and care for you?' Then the King will

THE SIMPLE SECRET STUDY GUIDE

answer, 'I tell you the truth, anything you did for even the least of my people here, you also did for me.'"[1]

I think about the ways that I see people around me.

My coworker with a long, painful illness.

My neighbor facing another surgery.

My neighbor who practices a faith that does not look like mine.

The woman in the retirement community who rarely has visitors.

A student who has lost his way in getting a degree.

A friend who reveals she is struggling with depression.

A childhood friend who is dealing with her aging mother.

The younger friend investing in her faith, her career, her children, and her husband.

A person struggling with gender identity in our world shouting so many opinions.

The child on the playground who consistently annoys other children.

I want to see these humans, made in God's image, and love them as Jesus did. It's easy for me to see how Jesus loved people in the first century. I could do that, right? Love the people that Jesus loved? I could see him do it and do the same.

The disciples living and walking beside Jesus had challenges loving some people. Like the tax collector. The guy who cheated them by charging them more than the tax law required to keep some for himself. Jesus invited one of these shady guys to be in his inner circle, too.[2]

Women. Jesus saw women. He valued women in a culture where they were considered property and only valuable if they could bear sons. Jesus announced his ministry to a woman. A woman who was a Samaritan, had been married many times, and was living with another man, not her husband.[3]

---

1. Matt 25:35–40 (New Century Version).

2. Matt 9:9–13.

3. John 4:1–42.

LOVING HUMANS

Would I be able to love the people Jesus loved? It is easy to say over two thousand years later. I know the story. I know about Jesus' three-year ministry, his trial, his crucifixion, and how the disciples were crushed. Jesus did not become a warrior, a military leader that would overtake the Roman oppression as the Jews had hoped. I know why. He was raised on the third day to be the atonement for my sins and the world's sins. I know this. It is easier to believe, knowing the whole story and not living in fear that he was gone with all of my hopes and dreams for our Savior.

He loved people. All people—ones that were downcast, demon-filled, cheaters, poor in spirit. Disappointed people, people who felt betrayed. Could I love as Jesus did? Would I have loved like Jesus?

In my work, I have the opportunity to meet incredible people. I hosted a speaker for the Christian University Distinguished Speaker series one day. At this college, this woman was not as well known by her name, Ruby Bridges, as she was known for the Norman Rockwell painting depicting her, *The Problem We All Live With*.

That night, she told the story of her six-year-old self—walking into Franz Elementary School every day—while white people screamed and harassed her for desegregating the school. Parents took their kids out of school; she was the only student in her class that year. One day, the school psychiatrist saw her talking to these adults who were shouting at her as she walked into the building. When she entered the classroom, the psychiatrist nervously asked Ruby what she was saying to them. Her reply was, "I am not talking to them. I am praying for them because they don't know what they are doing."[4] That is love. She loved humans.

The Problem We All Live With: The image of six-year-old Ruby Bridges bravely walking into school, escorted by four US Marshals and greeted by mobs protesting the integration of an elementary school in New Orleans in November 1960.

"I wasn't talking. I was praying. I was praying for them." That is love. Loving humans.

---

4. Bridges, *Through My Eyes*.

THE SIMPLE SECRET STUDY GUIDE

I heard Ruby's story of innocence, courage, and forgiveness. I heard her share her story with television journalists, print journalists, and a packed campus auditorium. I saw her sincerity, kindness, and goodness each time. Children, college students, parents, and grandparents came together to hear her story. If you listened to her story, you changed to see the good, to be the good. Goodness isn't a color, and goodness doesn't see color. Goodness looks for goodness.

I felt at ease with her like you do with a longtime friend. I was with her when she said, "It isn't Black History Month; it is just history, our American history. One that should be told every day." I've always thought the same thing. What she did those days in 1960, she did for all children. She did it for me, my children, and my future grandchildren.

Be like Ruby Bridges. Look for goodness.

Six-year-old Ruby Bridges loved these humans by praying for them. *Every villain, stranger, enemy, and adversary is my neighbor waiting to be transformed by love.*[5] Ruby teaches us how she chose to love and continue to love people despite themselves.

Ruby loved the rioting crowds in 1960; today, people are different. Harder to love. Right?

Journal:

- In your life, who are people that are difficult to love?
- Name the ones that are most challenging for you.
- What can you do to show love in these challenging relationships?

5. Graves, *Simple Secret*, 33.

4

Loving Myself

As an Enneagram One, loving myself does not come easy. I believe in it—for other people. But I have to schedule a time to love myself. I am good at planning things and keeping my calendar; however, it feels selfish to take time for self-care. I have learned that I am a better me when I do.

Several years ago, I took a deep dive into studying the Enneagram. It was a gift to myself to understand and give language in ways I was different from my close family and friends. My husband had figured out some of this before we had this language. He realized I spent my free time working on projects and lists at home and was much more relaxed away from home. As a Seven, he wanted to have spontaneous weekend trips, and I would prefer to spend a Saturday cleaning out a closet or the home office. Through my study of the Enneagram, I realized that my way was not the only right way. It's hard to admit because my way seemed pretty *right*.

Honestly, the Enneagram gave me perspective on a deeper understanding of myself, on loving myself for the way God made me, and on getting a glimpse into how my loved ones operated.

"You shall love your neighbor as yourself." The first assumption is that you love yourself.

THE SIMPLE SECRET STUDY GUIDE

"Forget about the wrong things people do to you, and do not try to get even. Love your neighbor as you love yourself. I am the Lord."[1]

Jesus said, "Love the Lord your God with all your heart, all your soul, and all your mind. This is the first and most important command. And the second command is like the first: 'Love your neighbor as you love yourself."[2]

Love ourselves. The Old Testament and New Testament both emphasize this. Love God and love people.

> May you recognize in your life the presence, power, in light of your soul. May you realize that you are never alone and that your soul and its brightness and belonging connect you intimately with the rhythm of the universe. May you have respect for your individuality and difference. They realize that the shape of your soul is unique and, that you have a splendid destiny here, and that behind the façade of your life, there is something beautiful and eternal happening. But you learn to see yourself with the same delight, pride, and expectation with which God sees you in every moment.[3]

Journal:

- Why is it important to love yourself?
- What do you do for self-care?
- How can you be more intentional about scheduling time for self-care to be healthy and show love to yourself?
- How do you invest in yourself to be the best version of yourself?

1. Lev 19:18 (NCV).
2. Matt 22:37–39 (NCV).
3. Cron and Stabile, *Road Back to You,* 230.

5

Loving Partners

Josh opens this chapter with a quote from *New York Times* contributor Alain de Botton about his writings on why we will marry the wrong person. Have you ever felt like you married the wrong person?

"Until you know yourself, you can't possibly relate to another person."[1]

So much of loving ourselves—finding and developing that language to communicate feeling loved—relates to loving our partners. Brené Brown shares a story[2] of being disappointed with her husband for not celebrating her birthday to her expectations. Brown shared that with her therapist, who asked: "Did you share with your husband what your expectations were?" Brown responded that it would not be worth it if she had to tell him what to do. The therapist replied, "If you're not asking for what's important to you, maybe it's because you don't think *you* are worth it."

Communicating our expectations to our partners makes us feel vulnerable but brave. Opening this meaningful way to communicate leads to mutual conversations to share ways to love and receive love.

---

1. de Botton, "Why You Will Marry the Wrong Person."
2. Brown, *Atlas of the Heart*, 47.

THE SIMPLE SECRET STUDY GUIDE

Why are we nicer to strangers than the one person we committed to love for the rest of our lives? Is it because a stranger won't question your reason for leaving the mess in the bathroom, an unmade bed, etc.?

"When you love someone, you do not love them all the time, in the same way, from moment to moment. It is an impossibility. It is even a lie to pretend to. And yet, this is exactly what most of us demand. We have so little faith in the ebb and flow of life, of love, of relationships."[3]

I get up at 4:47 AM daily, which means Brett (and most people in my time zone) get up after me each day. He knows I appreciate the bed being made. If I have an early morning and leave before my husband is up, I will come home to a made bed with all the pillows in place. Does he care about the bed like that? No. He knows I do. I have said he will never make the bed if he lives longer than me. He does it for me. It's a way that he shows love because my love language is Acts of Service.[4] He makes me think of ways to show my love to him. His love language is Quality Time.[5] This shows up in watching a Netflix series, lingering after a meal, or watching TikTok with him. I am only sometimes good at it. My Enneagram One brain does not rest easily and wants to work. Learning about these differences helps me in intentionally invest in our relationship and understand that all brains are not wired as a One (although other Ones may agree with me).

Investing in ways to understand yourself through Enneagram[6] or *The Five Love Languages,*[7] for example, gives you language to express yourself and have insight into your partner—ultimately, to be the best version of yourself. To take a deeper dive into this investment into fully living with your partner and understanding how your personalities are created, Susanne Stabile, in *The Path Between Us*, gives meaning to the motivations and dynamics

3. Lindberg, *Gift from the Sea*, 12.

4. Chapman, *Five Love Languages.*

5. Chapman, *Five Love Languages.*

6. Cron and Stabile, *Road Back to You.*

7. Chapman, *Five Love Languages.*

16

LOVING PARTNERS

of our partners and provides us with a tool to develop healthy relationships.[8]

Journal:

- How are you better because of your husband/wife?
- How do you want your partner to see you love him/her?
- What is a way you communicate how you feel loved to your partner?
- How is your husband/wife better because of you?

If unmarried, use these prompts:

- How will you be better because of someone you love?
- How will you want someone you love to see you love him or her?
- How will you communicate to someone you love how you feel loved?
- How will someone you love be better because of you?

---

8 Stabile, *Path Between Us.*

6

Loving Children

Josh is a gifted writer about loving our children. If your season of life has reached having children, you can relate to how beautifully written this love for our children is. This chapter mentions a powerful testimony from Trent Dilfer, and it is worth your time and will leave you changed. Josh said it is the most downloaded podcast of all time at his church.[1]

This chapter may also be painful— if you have struggled with infertility and dream of loving a child, are yearning to reconcile with a child, or are living with relationship consequences from poor choices.

Our grandson is almost two years old and loves trucks and all vehicles. Our daughter sent a sweet video of Harry watching a tractor clip the other day. He said, "Tractor! Love you, tractor." I adored the sweetness of Harry learning our language and the pure expression of his love for tractors. (We need options for expressing *love* in our languages, as discussed in chapter 2.) It is so beautiful when our children are developing speech and speaking the thoughts they are experiencing. Their language is pure and unfiltered.

---

1. Dilfer, "Letting Go of Fear."

LOVING CHILDREN

As we mature, we develop a filter for keeping these thoughts to ourselves. This filter is good in many ways but can also limit relationships.

Josh uses two stories to show how we love our children: Abraham and Isaac and the parable of the prodigal son. Both stories are told in Sunday school and Vacation Bible School. We hear them, tell them, and remember them.

Read: Abraham and Issac.[2]

As a parent, I view Abraham's story quite differently than I did as a child. I do not remember hearing it the first time and worrying about Isaac. I knew God would take care of it, as Abraham told Isaac, "God will provide for the sacrifice."

As a parent of four adult children, three of whom are now parents themselves, I wonder if I have put my children before God. Wasn't that what God was testing? Did Abraham love Isaac more than he loved the Lord God? How would I complete the test if God measured my love for him vs. my love for my son or daughter?

Read the parable of the prodigal son.[3]

I have two brothers. They challenged my parents in their teen years. You could align their journeys with the prodigal son's journey in separate seasons. Although neither brother asked my parents for their inheritance, they lived recklessly. Once, my mother compared me to the older brother, saying I never caused my parents any trouble. I remember feeling uneasy with the compliment. I saw the older brother in the parable as resentful and unhappy. Was I bitter and sad?

Which son would describe your relationship with your parents as when you lived under their roof? As a parent welcoming your lost son or daughter home, have you forgotten the faithful daughter or son? Loving our children is complicated, sometimes challenging, and wonderfully fulfilling.

Our love for our children is a mystery, and "as we have multiple children, love is not divided, love is multiplied."[4]

2. Gen 22:1–19.

3. Luke 15:11–32.

4. Graves, *Simple Secret*, 68.

THE SIMPLE SECRET STUDY GUIDE

We experience a glimpse of our Father's love for us when we have our first child. The overwhelming power of love fills our hearts—our hearts explode. The miracle happens when we have the second, third, and fourth; our hearts grow and have as much love for each of these sweet souls. We experience something like the love God has for all of humanity. It is overwhelming to comprehend how God loves each one of the eight billion people on planet Earth and exponentially the billions of people since Adam and Eve. "Only love can be divided endlessly and still not diminish," as Anne Morrow Lindberg wrote so beautifully.[5]

Journal:

- When was a time when I loved my child/children more than my love for God?

- What prodigal son story role did I have in my family: the younger or older son?

- How can I be satisfied with my past and forgive myself for taking on the younger son's recklessness or the older son's pious attitude and dissatisfaction?

5. Lindbergh, *Gift from the Sea*, 24.

7

Loving Friends

Jesus was teaching in a house. The crowds were enormous. A paralyzed man had friends who took him to see Jesus. They carried him on his cot. This story is familiar.

In Luke 2:20, when Jesus saw their faith, he said, "Friend, your sins are forgiven." Much of the focus is on the Pharisees' reaction to Jesus having the power and authority[1] to forgive sins. The word that stands out to me is *friend*. This man was carried to Jesus by his friends. These friends did not give up when getting to Jesus was not readily accessible. They went through the roof and lowered the man down right before Jesus. *The Chosen* has a powerful scene of this event.[2] Who is your circle of friends who would carry you to Jesus if needed? Who would you carry to Jesus, and who would tear out the roof to bring you to Jesus?

I work in the nonprofit healthcare industry, specifically a hospice foundation. I was given a new hospice book by a colleague. The book's content centers around hospice but is more about relationships and how they change us.

The book is *The In-Between: Unforgettable Encounters During Life's Final Moments,* by Hadley Vlahos. Nurse Hadley describes

---

1. Luke 5:17–39 and Mark 2:1–12.
2 *Chosen*, season 1, episode 6.

THE SIMPLE SECRET STUDY GUIDE

twelve patients and how they changed her life. Our friends change us, and we change them.

Hadley was assigned a new patient, Lily, one day. When Hadley arrived at the patient's home, she found Lily and Allison. It turns out that they were friends staying at the rented beach house, which gave Lily one more chance to have her feet in the sand.

Lily was struggling, and Alison was exasperated about what to do. Lily was in hospice care in her hometown and called the beach town hospice for care on this trip. When they arrived, Lily was declining and too weak to walk out on the sand. While Hadley was doing her patient assessment, Alison slipped out. Hadley looked up to see Alison returning to the condo with a pan of sand she had collected from the shore. Alison was determined to have Lily's feet in the sand—even if that meant bringing the sand to her. "Then it was as if the universe knew, and the wind stopped along with Lily's breath. All was silent for a moment before Allison's sobs filled the room."[3]

Hadley saw these two women's love and friendship and reflected on her friendships. Hadley finished up her work and left the condo. She knew what she needed to do. Hadley called her lifelong friend, who lived many miles away, and invited her to be a bridesmaid. Do not wait to bridge a friendship that has been important in our life.

Our friends change us, and we change them.

Journal:

- Who in your circle of friends would carry you to Jesus if needed?

- Who would you carry and tear out the roof to bring to Jesus?

- What friend would you take to put her feet in the sand one last time?

- Who needs to know what their friendship has meant to you?

3. Vlahos, *In-Between*, 173.

8

Loving the Vulnerable

In my world, I have the opportunity to give gifts of kindness and experiences to people receiving hospice care through the generosity of our donors. While writing this study guide, my team gave a twelve-year-old girl with a brain tumor and her family an experience at Magic Springs, a local amusement park in Arkansas. Our team delivering this experience consisted of her social worker, her RN, our communication director, and me. Our two caregivers emulated loving the vulnerable so beautifully. Each of our caregivers was gifted with compassion for our young patient and her large family of ten. In rural Arkansas, generational poverty exists widely. Several dogs met us while walking to this family's modest trailer home. We met the family on the porch to make the presentation. Our RN reminded us that our patient had shared her dreams about what she wanted to do this summer. This twelve-year-old girl, a rising seventh grader with a recent brain cancer diagnosis, could not imagine her state in a few weeks and requested an amusement park visit for her family. Isn't that what all twelve-year-olds should be wishing for? I had a lump in my throat throughout the entire presentation and time with this family.

I watched the mom and dad enjoy the moment with their daughter as she was excited to begin planning the trip. Our RN did the medical assessment, and an older sister prepared lunch.

THE SIMPLE SECRET STUDY GUIDE

I could see the ache in the father's eyes, knowing he could not change this diagnosis and was doing all he could to provide treatment for his young daughter with not much time to live, to love her. This is vulnerability.

This family lives each day in the precious time that has been so drastically cut short for their daughter—a rising seventh grader who likely will not see the first day of junior high, only two months away. How do we love people like this? How do you love them? How can you see the vulnerable in your world? James admonishes us to be doers of the word (James 1).

"Do Something,"[1] a song by Matthew West, simplifies James. You may want to give it a listen.

I witnessed the beautiful, gifted caregivers who daily love people with life-limiting diagnoses and helped them live their lives to the fullest—whatever that may be.

We may be paralyzed when thinking about the millions of vulnerable people around us. We can do something for one of these vulnerable people, loving her and caring for him. James says it boldly. Consider two different translations:

"Religion that God our Father accepts as pure and faultless is this: to look after orphans and widows in their distress and to keep oneself from being polluted by the world."[2]

"Religion that God accepts as pure and without fault is this: caring for the orphans or widows who need help and keeping yourself free from the world's influence."[3]

Reading different versions can have more profound meaning when contemplating the charge of our religion to be pure and faultless.

---

1. Matthew West, "Do Something," track 4 on *Into the Light*, Sparrow, 2012.
2. Jas 1:27 (NIV).
3. Jas 1:27 (NCV).

LOVING THE VULNERABLE

Journal:

- Our job is to love others without stopping to inquire whether they are worthy.

- How can you love one vulnerable person?[4]

- What *something* will you do?

4. Graves, *Simple Secret*, 90.

9

Loving the Poor

As we grow up, we dream about what our lives will be like. No one dreams of being poor. If we enter the world in a lower-income family, we still aspire to be middle class at least. Josh opens this chapter with the four myths of our deepest desires.[1]

- Myth #1: I am what I do (work and vocation).
- Myth #2: I am what others think and say about me (perception).
- Myth #3: I am what I have (materialism and consumerism).
- Myth #4: I am mostly satisfied when I am comfortable (security).

No one wants to be poor. No one wants the shame of it.

The story of Lazarus is about these same things.[2]

Wealth has hardened the rich man's heart, and he does not feel compassion for the man begging outside his gate. This man does not leverage his wealth to love the people he encounters daily.

My work in a nonprofit foundation allows me to see how people can give generously to help others. Our office gets regular calls from our social workers requesting help for hospice patients'

---

1. Graves, *Simple Secret*, 96.
2. Luke 16: 19–31.

LOVING THE POOR

nonmedical needs. Requests for food, clothing, and other essentials like wheelchair access, funeral expenses, and assistance with utility bills are the types of requests that come across my desk. A generous family started a fund to cover these basics and regularly gives to continue to fund these types of requests.

We call these Gifts of Kindness—kindness, love, anonymous love for low-income people. My role is minimal in granting these requests; however, it is a blessing for me to work with so many generous people and help them steward their resources to love the poor. I have called donors when a unique request comes in and immediately heard, "Yes, I want to help."

Seeing this generosity has given me the freedom to adopt that same attitude. "Yes, I want to help." Each of us is blessed in many different ways, and how we choose to love the poor with our time, talent, and treasure is our response to how God has blessed each of us.

A favorite book that helps give perspective on giving and planning to give is *When Women Give,* by Kim King. She writes, "We have the responsibility for financial decisions and resources— or we will. God wouldn't place resources in our hands if he wouldn't provide for us to be wise stewards."[3]

Journal:

- Which myth is the most difficult for you to ignore?

    - Myth #1: I am what I do (work and vocation).

    - Myth #2: I am what others think and say about me (perception).

    - Myth #3: I am what I have (materialism and consumerism).

    - Myth #4: I am mostly satisfied when I am comfortable (security).

- How can one avoid having the rich man's attitude and ignoring the poor?

3. King, *When Women Give,* 43.

The Simple Secret Study Guide

- What plans do you make to provide resources to help your community's poor? Giving generously helps the beneficiary; gifting time, talent, and treasures blesses the benefactor exponentially.

10

Loving Strangers

In the intro to this chapter, Josh uses Malcolm Gladwell's work to show how our interactions with strangers can be life-changing. The audio version of his book, *Talking to Strangers*,[1] is so powerful, as Gladwell styles his book like his acclaimed podcast, *Revisionist History*,[2] and gives the reader so much more than the book already does. *Talking to Strangers* was the first book my new book club read together. It was the first time I realized and contemplated our interactions with strangers.

How do you interact with strangers? We encounter them so often. My husband, Brett, is gifted in loving strangers. One of the things I noticed about him when we met in college was how he treated everyone with respect and love. We often had people on the fringe joining us in the student center for an encouraging word. Even at a Christian college, people feel isolated, unwelcome in the "cool" groups/clubs, and alone. Brett has a way of seeing people like this and drawing them in. He uses his social media to praise the regular fast-food worker, deli server, barista, or sanitation

---

1. Gladwell, *Talking to Strangers*.
2. Gladwell, *Revisionist History*, podcast.

THE SIMPLE SECRET STUDY GUIDE

employee.[3] Watching him helps me see ordinary people and see that they deserve love like I do.

Our twin daughters had several opportunities to be flower girls at weddings. We lived in a college town and developed relationships with college students. At one wedding rehearsal, there was an announcement that the preacher could not attend because his fifteen-year-old nephew suddenly died of an undetected heart complication. I had been looking forward to seeing that preacher and did not know his extended family.

A few years later, Oprah had a hairstylist from Missouri on her show. It turns out this woman was the mother of the fifteen-year-old son that had died suddenly. In her grief, she and her husband took a long weekend trip to New York City. That weekend, on the front page of the *New York Times*, there was a picture of a boy named Mark, an eight-year-old living in Ghana as an enslaved child. This grief-stricken mother could not get Mark off her mind and eventually made a trip to Ghana. She rescued Mark and ten other children from slavery.

That same morning, Oprah also saw Mark's picture on the *New York Times* front page. Oprah sent one of her staff members to find Mark. When her staff member arrived in Ghana a few days later, she was *shocked* that someone had beaten her there. Oprah wanted to have this woman, Pam Cope, on her show to hear about her story and journey. What I loved about the story is that Pam is a regular person with regular resources, but she did something extraordinary because she saw a stranger who needed to be loved.[4]

Journal:

- How often are we frozen because we cannot solve all of the world's problems with child slavery, hunger, and generational poverty? That did not stop Pam. She wanted to help Mark. She did a remarkable thing to go to distant Ghana.

3. Thefriendinmind, Instagram.
4. Cope, *Jantsen's Gift.*

LOVING STRANGERS

- What is stopping you from loving a stranger?
- Can you find your Mark?

We often freeze in loving strangers because we cannot do all the work and love all the strangers. But we can love one stranger and do that well.

11

Loving Enemies

Loving enemies seems like an oxymoron. Enemies show up in our everyday lives.

Family enemies: Close family members who have betrayed us or harmed us.

Ex-friend enemies: Friends who have lost our trust and respect because of reckless actions.

Local enemies: People who belong to the "wrong" school or neighborhood and believe the "wrong" things.

National enemies: People of different ethnicities, socioeconomic tribes, and Dallas Cowboys football fans.

Global enemies: International religious rivals and nations that stand opposed to the best interests of the United States (e.g., China, Russia, Syria).[1]

Are you holding on to any of these enemies? Each one of our enemies is a child of God. Honestly, can I comprehend this love?

The good Samaritan parable suggests that a Samaritan, a supposed enemy of the Jewish people, could rise to the occasion of assisting an injured "neighbor." Americans do not feel hatred toward Samaritans. We do not know any. But what about people with different skin colors, political parties, and religions?

---

1. Graves, *Simple Secret,* 120.

LOVING ENEMIES

A few years ago, I would host four or five nationally known speakers each year in my work with a Christian university. I remember many things about the thirty-plus speakers I hosted over the six years of my work there, and I even made friends with a few. There were two I hosted that loved their enemies incredibly well. (See Ruby Bridges in chapter 3.)

About ten days before her lecture on campus, Eva Kor's story[2] on BuzzFeed had over 180 million views. Because of that, our auditorium was filled on the night of our event, likely breaking the fire code to hear Eva Kor. Eva was a Holocaust survivor and, with her twin, was a subject of unspeakable experimentation by Dr. Mengele. It is easy to see how Eva would consider Dr. Mengele her enemy. Her story,[3] about the power of forgiveness, is powerful, and meeting her changed me. Soon after her lecture, a documentary was made about her life, and there are several scenes from the night I hosted her in this film.

She was a remarkable woman, and I will not forget her forgiveness. "Forgive your worst enemy. It will heal your soul and set you free."[4]

Journal:

- Who do I consider my enemy?
- What burden do I bear hating my enemies?
- What is one change I can make to love one enemy?

2. McNeal, "Holocaust Survivor Has Written About Why She Shook a Former Nazi's Hand."

3. Kor, *Surviving the Angel of Death.*

4. Green, dir., *Eva: A-7063.*

12

Only Love Can Set You Free

Remember at the beginning of this study when we shared Oliver's wet kiss story and other stories about feeling completely loved? Over the chapters of this study guide, we have taken a deep dive into *The Simple Secret* and reflected on what loving God and loving people might look like in our lives. When we focus on something, God gives us opportunities to see that in real time.

While writing this study guide, I faced the challenges of my aging mother—her declining health, her estate dealings, and how members of my family dealt with these things differently. Over and over in my head, I heard, "*Love is a rugged commitment to be with someone, to be for someone, unto Christ's likeness, for as long as it takes.*"[1] This language gave me the mental and physical strength to handle what was needed. I was looking at my mother and hearing these words. While practicing this rugged commitment toward my mother, I received this rugged commitment of love.

Having my husband, Brett, encourage me and walk beside me on the most challenging days gave me the strength to push through. As an Enneagram One, I find strength and renewal in work and completing tasks. Preparing my parents' home for sale seemed daunting, and I felt paralyzed about what to do. Brett

1. Graves, *Simple Secret*, 5.

ONLY LOVE CAN SET YOU FREE

stepped in and managed many tasks difficult for me to execute. Life is beautiful and challenging at the same time.

Share a time when this *rugged commitment to be with someone, to be for someone unto Christ's likeness*, challenged you. Where are you now in loving those around you?

Priya Parker's *The Art of Gathering* explores why meeting with our communities is crucial to fulfilling lives. We are designed to love those around us, and it matters to grow in communities. We need meaningful and memorable experiences. "We all wear masks, and while masks have been used, taking them off can allow for deeper connection, shared growth, and more fruitful collaboration."[2]

Another author reflects on our humanity and how we love. Thomas Merton's posthumously published work *Love and Living* describes the start of love as the decision to allow those we love to be entirely themselves without attempting to mold them to fit our own image. If our love is based on their potential to become more like us, we do not truly love them—we only love the reflection of ourselves that we see in them. You don't need to know exactly what is happening or where it's all headed. What matters is recognizing the opportunities and challenges of the present moment and facing them with courage, faith, and hope.[3]

> Every time we make the decision to love someone, we open ourselves to great suffering because those we most love cause us not only great joy but also great pain. The greatest pain comes from leaving. When the child leaves home, when the husband or wife leaves for a long period or for good, and when the beloved friend departs to another country or dies . . . the pain of leaving can tear us apart. Still, if we want to avoid the suffering of leaving, we will never experience the joy of loving. And love is stronger than fear, life stronger than death, hope stronger than despair. We have to trust that the risk of loving is always worth taking.[4]

2. Parker, *Art of Gathering*, 58.

3. Merton, *Love and Living*.

4. Nouwen, *Return of the Prodigal Son*, 91–92.

THE SIMPLE SECRET STUDY GUIDE

We have focused this study on loving God, ourselves, and the people around us. For a moment, contemplate how you let God love you, your partner, your children, and everyone around you.

During COVID-19, our twin daughters were each expecting their first babies. Our first granddaughter was born, and we did not meet her until she came home from the hospital. A few weeks later, my husband and I waited for our first grandson in a small coffee shop. Our daughter had been in labor for thirty-six hours, and it was difficult not to worry. We had been chatting with an older couple that morning when I stepped away to take a call from my son-in-law to say that the doctor recommended a C-section for delivery. I returned to the table, overcome with emotions. The woman asked if she could pray for us and our daughter. My tears freely flowed while listening to the beautiful prayer for a healthy delivery and for us to be free from worry. What a blessing that was. Strangers act on the Holy Spirit's nudging to help calm our nerves, give us hope, and love us. We both felt loved by our Father and by this couple that walked into our lives briefly that morning.

Journal:

- Which love relationship has been most effortless for you? (God, humans, self, partner, children, friends, the vulnerable, the poor, strangers, enemies, siblings, or your parents.)

- Which love relationship has been the most challenging?

- What are you planning to do to love those around you? Pick one person you know and develop a plan for loving them. After all, no plans will be plans for no results.

Bonus Chapter: Loving Parents

As our parents age, we are transformed into the role that they earlier played in our lives. Their health may decline, and their need for help grows. This transition can be smooth and readily accepted or rocky and resisted, however much needed.

My full-of-life, strong, healthy seventy-five-year-old father was unexpectedly diagnosed with bladder cancer. After an eighteen-month journey with treatment, he left his earthly home. My daddy was the one we thought would outlive us all. He had been the picture of health, took no daily medication, and would rarely need Tylenol. He was a fierce protector of family and helper to all (textbook Enneagram Two). If I called him at any time of the day or night and asked, "Daddy, what are you doing?," his always enthusiastic response was "What do you need me to do?"

What I needed ranged from running a car pool for our four children, babysitting our dogs if we went on a soccer trip, meeting me for lunch to hear about my world, removing a pet rabbit that may not have survived, and much more.

I remember walking into church to join our parents in our pew—a little late. I wanted to slip in as quietly as possible. ("Slipping in" with four children is easier said than done.) My daddy was highly excited to see our family *whenever* he saw them. As they walked past him to their seat, he hugged and kissed each one. I remember pausing one Sunday to think *this* would not always be possible. People do not live forever, although we all thought he might.

THE SIMPLE SECRET STUDY GUIDE

It made a small scene sitting in the balcony that morning. I am sure some looked endearingly, and some had other disagreeable thoughts. However, that Sunday, I chose to cherish the moment.

My mother became a widow on April 19, 2014, after nearly fifty years of marriage. That day, my role began to change. First, I became a teacher. Teaching is a role I love and have years of experience in. Teaching your parents is different. I taught my parents how to use technology. But now I was teaching my mother how to pay bills, where she banked, why you need an oil change, and much besides. My daddy had been a protector and helper who did everything behind the scenes. But Mother adapted well and soon was running the household like a pro.

I always smiled when I got her call. "Do you know how much an oil change costs?" Why yes, I do. I have been adulting for over thirty years.

As time passed, my mother needed more help with household maintenance, managing money, and eventually moving from home into an independent living community. Although it is written in one sentence above, the transition in each way she needed help went differently than learning to run a household.

Many times in our conversations, I have heard, "Kim thinks she's my mother." or "You are not my boss!"

Navigating the journey of changing roles is not for the faint of heart. Separating feelings from the necessary changes through love is challenging. I have reassured and encouraged myself with these words: "Love is a rugged commitment to be with someone, for someone, unto Christlikeness, for as long as it takes."

And as Josh writes, "Love is the daily decision to be tenaciously aware and attentive of the needs around you."

When Jesus saw his mother and the follower he loved standing nearby, he said to his mother, "Dear woman, here is your son." Then he said to the follower, "Here is your mother." From then on, the follower took her to live in his home.[1]

Roles change. Love remains.

---

1. John 19:26–27.

BONUS CHAPTER: LOVING PARENTS

Journal:

- In what ways do you show love to your parents?
- What is a challenging part of your relationship with your parents?
- Which parent has been easier to love?
- Which one has been more difficult?
- Blended families add complexity to this changing role of parent and child; in what ways do additional parents influence you?

Bibliography

Bridges, Ruby. *Through My Eyes*. New York: Scholastic, 1999.

Brooks, Arthur. *From Strength to Strength*. New York: Penguin, 2022.

Brown, Brené. *Atlas of the Heart*. New York: Penguin Random House, 2021.

Chapman, Gary D. *The Five Love Languages*. Chicago: Walker Large Print, 2010.

Chapman, Gary, and Chris Shuler. *Life-Changing Cross-Cultural Friendships*. Grand Rapids: Zondervan, 2022.

Cope, Pam. *Jantsen's Gift: A True Story of Grief, Rescue, and Grace*. New York: Grand Central, 2011.

Cron, Ian Morgan, and Suzanne Stabile. *The Road Back to You*. Downers Grove, IL: InterVarsity, 2016.

Crouch, Andy. "The Life We're Looking For: Reclaiming Relationships in a Technological World." *Perspectives on Science and Christian Faith* 75, no. 1 (2023) 72–74. https://doi.org/10.56315/pscf3–23crouch.

de Botton, Alain. "Why You Will Marry the Wrong Person." *The New York Times*, May 28, 2016. https://www.nytimes.com/2016/05/29/opinion/sun day/why-you-will-marry-the-wrong-person.html?smid=url-share.

Dilfer, Trent. "Letting Go of Fear: The Fear of Losing Someone Precious." Sermon, Otter Creek Church, July 28, 2019. https://ottercreek.org/sermon/letting-go-of-fear-the-fear-of-losing-someone-precious/.

Gladwell, Malcolm. *Revisionist History*. Podcast. https://www.gladwellbooks.com/landing-page/malcom-gladwell-podcasts/.

———. *Talking to Strangers: What We Should Know About the People We Don't Know*. New York: Back Bay, 2021.

Goff, Bob. *Love Does*. Nashville: Thomas Nelson, 2012.

Goff, Maria. *Love Lives Here*. Nashville: B & H, 2017.

Gokey, Danny. "Love God and Love People." YouTube video, July 7, 2020, 5:03. https://youtu.be/cQ8D2Mx7tGg.

Graves, Joshua. *The Simple Secret*. Eugene, OR: Cascade, 2023.

Green, Ted, dir. *Eva: A-7063*. Indianapolis: WFYI Public Media and Ted Green Films, 2021.

King, Kimberly. *When Women Give*. Downers Grove, IL: InterVarsity, 2017.

Kor, Eva Mozes. *Surviving the Angel of Death: The True Story of a Mengele Twin in Auschwitz*. Terre Haute, IN: Tanglewood, 2020.

BIBLIOGRAPHY

Lindbergh, Anne Morrow. *Gift from the Sea*. New York: Pantheon, 1955.

McKnight, Scot. "The Four Elements of Love." Jesus Creed (blog), May 1, 2015. Patheos.com/blogs/jesuscreed/2015/05/01/the-four-elements-of-love/.

McNeal, Stephanie. "A Holocaust Survivor Has Written About Why She Shook a Former Nazi's Hand." BuzzFeed, April 26, 2015. https://www.pbs.org/video/eva-a-7062-educational-version-umfa2y/.

Merton, Thomas. *Love and Living*. Edited by Naomi Burton Stone and Brother Patrick Hart. New York: Harcourt Brace Jovanovich, 1979.

Nouwen, Henri J. M. *The Return of the Prodigal Son: A Story of Homecoming*. New York: Image, 1992.

Parker, Priya. *The Art of Gathering*. New York: Riverhead, 2018.

"*The Problem We All Live With*." Wikipedia. https://en.wikipedia.org/wiki/The_Problem_We_All_Live_With.

Rohr, Richard. *Essential Teachings on Love*. Edited by Joelle Chase and Judy Traeger. Maryknoll, NY: Orbis, 2018.

Stabile, Suzanne. *The Path Between Us*. Downers Grove, IL: InterVarsity, 2018.

Vlahos, Hadley. *The In-Between: Unforgettable Encounters During Life's Final Moments*. New York: Ballantine, 2023.

www.ingramcontent.com/pod-product-compliance
Lightning Source LLC
Chambersburg PA
CBHW022125040426
42450CB00006B/860